You Were Worth the Wait

Written by **Stephanie & Alex Booe**

Illustrated by Aleksandra Szmidt

You Were Worth the Wait

Published by Wisdom House Books, Inc.
Chapel Hill, North Carolina 27514 USA • 1.919.883.4669
www.wisdomhousebooks.com

Wisdom House Books is committed to excellence in the publishing industry.
Book design copyright © 2020 by Wisdom House Books, Inc.
All rights reserved.

Cover and Interior Illustration by Aleksandra Szmidt
Cover and Interior design by Ted Ruybal
Published in the United States of America
Hardback ISBN: 978-1-7347872-0-7
LCCN: 2020907295

JNF019040 | JUVENILE NONFICTION / Family / New Baby
JNF019060 | JUVENILE NONFICTION / Family / Parents
JNF024090 | JUVENILE NONFICTION / Health & Daily Living / Sexuality & Pregnancy

First Edition

25 24 23 22 21 20 / 10 9 8 7 6 5 4 3 2 1

Dedication

A story of our baby, for our baby,
and dedicated to all of the couples
that know the various hardships
of building a family.

Not every family is the same.

Some are tall,
some are short.

Some families have a lot of children . . .

. . . and others don't have any at all.

Each of these families are special
in their own way and if you ask us,
ours was made just right!

Our sweet child,
this is the story of you.

We have been waiting for you for a long time. Long before you were even born!

We asked for a baby,
but it wasn't yet time to meet you.

While we thought it was the perfect time, it turns out we needed to learn a few things so we could be ready for all the amazing things you would do!

You would be a leader,
so we needed to learn how to listen.

You would be gentle,
so we needed to learn how to see
the good in every day.

You would make us laugh,
so we needed to learn how to smile.

You would be creative,
so we needed to learn how to
build things that matter.

You would be fearless,
so we needed to learn how to
have courage and bravery.

You would be so kind,
so we needed to learn how to
love others well.

You would change the world,
so we needed to learn how to
stand and fight for you.

You were perfect all along;
it was us that had to learn.
We spent our time waiting and we
spent our time learning so we could
embrace you—all of you!

And you, my sweet babe,
you were worth the wait.

About The Authors
Stephanie & Alex Booe

Meet Stephanie and Alex Booe. Two crazy kids that just wanted a child of their own. They got married in 2015 and started trying for children in 2017. In 2018, they received the hard truth of hearing infertility for the first time and found out that this would be their path. After five failed IUIs, they chose to pursue IVF in 2019. After a very successful first round of IVF, they were blessed to hear they would be welcoming their first child into the world in April of 2020. Their story is not one of easy paths, full of joyous moments. It is one of hardship and persistence. In the midst of their trials, they wrote this book. A tangible piece of hope for others going through similar situations of building a family.

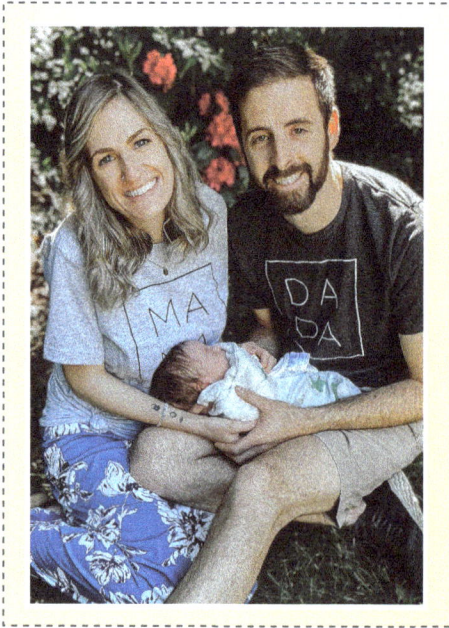

About The Illustrator
Aleksandra Szmidt

Aleksandra Szmidt grew up in a town in the south of Poland and currently resides in New Zealand. In Poland, she worked as a graphic designer. Upon moving, she decided to pursue her dream as a freelance illustrator. From her home studio, Aleksandra creates one-of-a-kind artwork for clients across the world. Her love of drawing plants and animals is attributed to her landscape architecture studies. However, she prefers to design magical things often detached from reality. She loves both traditional and digital painting, so she also likes to mix them. This brings her immense joy and an emotional connection to her artwork.

www.ingramcontent.com/pod-product-compliance
Lightning Source LLC
Chambersburg PA
CBHW040244100426
42811CB00011B/1147